DARKIE'S GIFT

THE STORY OF BOB, MARGARET AND DARKIE

CORRINE APOSTOLOPOULOU

Copyright © 2025 Corrine Apostolopoulou.

All rights reserved. No part of this book may be reproduced, stored, or transmitted by any means—whether auditory, graphic, mechanical, or electronic—without written permission of both publisher and author, except in the case of brief excerpts used in critical articles and reviews. Unauthorized reproduction of any part of this work is illegal and is punishable by law.

ISBN: 978-1-63950-388-9 (sc)
ISBN: 978-1-63950-390-2 (e)

Because of the dynamic nature of the Internet, any web addresses or links contained in this book may have changed since publication and may no longer be valid. The views expressed in this work are solely those of the author and do not necessarily reflect the views of the publisher, and the publisher hereby disclaims any responsibility for them.

Writers Apex

Gateway Towards Success

8063 MADISON AVE #1252
Indianapolis, IN 46227
+13176596889
www.writersapex.com

This is a true story about Margaret, Bob, and their dog, Darkie. Read through their life story and by buying the book, you can help others in similar situation to them.

This is Bob, Margaret and Darkie.

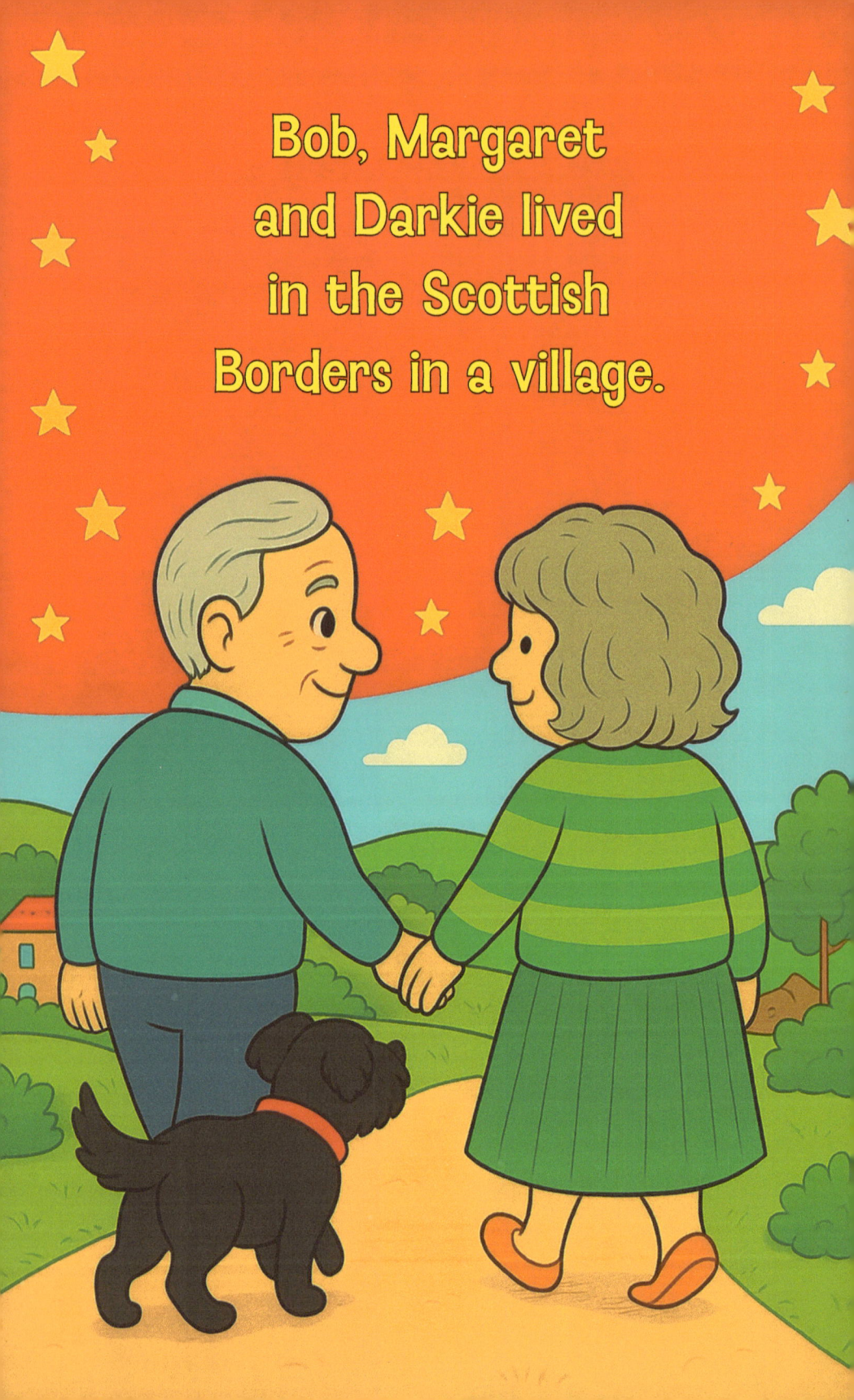

DEMENTIA

Dementia is an illness that affects how the brain works - including memory, understanding, judgment, language, and thinking. The most common type of dementia is known as Alzheimer's disease.

Dementia currently affects about 6% of people over 65 and 30% of people over 90, with more than 820,000 people living with the condition in the UK. By 2051, this number is expected to rise to 2 million. Around one-third of people with dementia live in care homes. The cost of care is estimated at £23 billion a year, and this could increase to £50 billion by 2039.

There are eight different types of dementia, but Alzheimer's disease remains the most common cause...

It was very difficult giving up their home where they had lived for many years but Margaret's dementia was getting worse and she kept forgetting things.

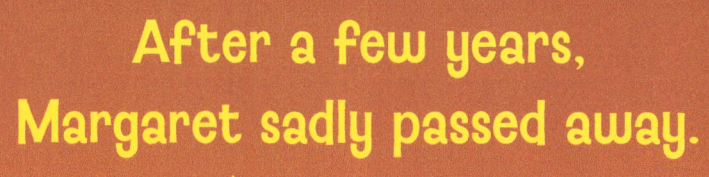

After a few years, Margaret sadly passed away.

New owners took over the care home where they lived, and they refused to allow the dog, Darkie, to stay there.

Bob was really sad, lonely and needed Darkie by his side, Bob decided he could never let Darkie leave him.

Bob was very worried about finding a new home where he and Darkie could stay together. Money was a problem because he only had his weekly pension.

Many people heard about Bob and Darkie's situation and wanted to help them.

A kind woman named Tracey started a petition to help Bob and his dog, Darkie, stay together—and more than 30,000 people signed it in support.

Their story appeared on television, radio, and in newspapers, touching the hearts of many who felt deep sympathy for them.

Bob and Darkie were even featured on *The Matthew Wright Show* in the UK, where many people heard about their story.

A crowdfunding page was also launched to help Bob and Darkie move to a new home, and generous donations soon poured in, raising thousands of pounds for their future care. Supporters of the petition even took their cause to 10 Downing Street in London, standing up for Bob and Darkie's right to stay together.

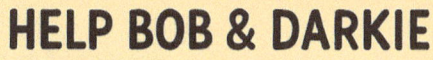

Bob and Darkie decided to move to a bungalow in Scotland so they could be closer to their relatives and friends and receive the support they needed, as Bob has to go to the hospital three times a week for treatments to stay healthy.

Bob and Darkie are now very happy living together in their bungalow, where they receive help from carers and others who assist with cleaning and sometimes cooking their meals. A wonderful organization called The Cinnamon Trust also helps by taking Darkie for walks, ensuring he gets plenty of fresh air and exercise.

Bob and Darkie are so grateful to have each other, sharing love, companionship, emotional support, and many funny moments together. Bob is especially thankful that he didn't have to part with his loyal dog, Darkie.

Bob feels a little worried about money, but he manages it carefully.

Having Darkie by his side remains the most important thing to him.

Corrine, who had previously fostered children and cared for adults with learning disabilities and illnesses, offered Bob and Darkie a room in her home. However, they chose to remain close to their elderly relatives and friends in Scotland. Deeply moved by their bond and circumstances, Corrine made a generous donation toward their care and later decided to write this book to help others in similar situations—especially those with beloved pets.

Now that Bob, Margaret, and their faithful dog Darkie have all passed away, this book is lovingly dedicated to their memory. Proceeds from its sale will be donated to five great causes that support others facing similar challenges.

Now that Bob and Darkie have passed away, it brings comfort to know that their story will continue to help others.

They would have wished that any proceed from this book— or if it is ever made into a movie— be given to these five great cause that bring hope, care, and compassion to both people and animals.

www.ingramcontent.com/pod-product-compliance
Lightning Source LLC
Chambersburg PA
CBHW041723070526
44585CB00001B/16